Hanukkah

FESTIVALS AROUND THE WORLD

Grace Jones

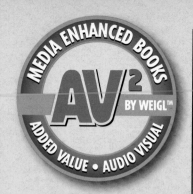

AV² provides enriched content that supplements and complements this book. Weigl's AV² books strive to create inspired learning and engage young minds in a total learning experience.

Your AV² Media Enhanced books come alive with...

Audio
Listen to sections of the book read aloud.

Key Words
Study vocabulary, and complete a matching word activity.

Video
Watch informative video clips.

Quizzes
Test your knowledge.

Embedded Weblinks
Gain additional information for research.

Slide Show
View images and captions, and prepare a presentation.

Try This!
Complete activities and hands-on experiments.

... and much, much more!

Go to **www.av2books.com**, and enter this book's unique code.

BOOK CODE

LBY83375

AV² by Weigl brings you media enhanced books that support active learning.

Published by AV² by Weigl
350 5ᵗʰ Avenue, 59ᵗʰ Floor   New York, NY 10118
Website: www.av2books.com

Library of Congress Cataloging-in-Publication Data

Names: Jones, Grace, 1990- author.
Title: Hanukkah / Grace Jones.
Description: New York, NY : AV2 by Weigl, [2018] I Series: Festivals around the world I Grades 4 to 6.
Identifiers: LCCN 2018003636 (print) I LCCN 2018004974 (ebook) I ISBN 9781489678065 (Multi User ebook) I ISBN 9781489678041 (hardcover : alk. paper) I ISBN 9781489678058 (softcover)
Subjects: LCSH: Hanukkah--Juvenile literature.
Classification: LCC BM695.H3 (ebook) I LCC BM695.H3 J66 2018 (print) I DDC 296.4/35--dc23
LC record available at https://lccn.loc.gov/2018003636

Printed in the United States of America in Brainerd, Minnesota
1 2 3 4 5 6 7 8 9 0 22 21 20 19 18

032017
120417

Project Coordinator: Heather Kissock   Designer: Ana María Vidal

First published in by Book Life in 2017

Weigl acknowledges Getty Images, Alamy, Shutterstock, and iStock as the primary image suppliers for this title.

Hanukkah

FESTIVALS AROUND THE WORLD

Hello, my name is Jacob.

When you see Jacob, he will tell you how to say a word.

Contents

What Is a Festival?

A festival takes place when people come together to celebrate a special event or time of the year. Some festivals last for only one day and others go on for many months.

Some people celebrate festivals by having a party with their family and friends. Others celebrate by holding special events, performing dances or playing music.

Jacob says:
SIN-A-GOG (Synagogue)
RAB-EYE (Rabbi)

The word
"**rabbi**" means
teacher
in Hebrew.

6

What Is Judaism?

Judaism is a religion that began around four thousand years ago in the Middle East. Jewish people believe in one God who they pray to in a synagogue or a Jewish place of worship.

Jewish people read a holy book called the Torah. The Torah sets out God's laws which instruct people on how to practice their faith. A rabbi uses the Torah to teach Jewish people about God's word.

What Is Hanukkah?

Hanukkah is a festival celebrated by Jewish people for eight days in November or December of every year. Jewish people are members of a religion called Judaism.

Jewish people come together to celebrate a time in history when they fought to practice their own religion. They celebrate by lighting special candles, playing games and eating fried food.

Hanukkah is also called the "**Festival of Lights**."

Jacob says:
HAN-U-KAH
(Hanukkah)

The Story of Hanukkah

A long, long time ago there was a great Greek king called Antiochus. He wanted the Jewish people to worship many Greek gods instead of their own God. Antiochus turned their Jewish temple into a place of worship for Zeus, one of the Greek gods.

They were very afraid of what the cruel king would do to them if they refused. One day a group of people, called the Maccabees, decided they wanted their temple back so they could worship their own God. The Maccabees bravely fought against the king's army and won.

Jacob says:
ANT-I-OKE-US
(Antiochus)
MAC-A-BEES
(Maccabees)

They returned to the temple and lit an oil lamp to cleanse the building of the Greek gods. They wanted to burn the lamp for eight days, but they only had a tiny drop of oil left. They lit the oil and eight days later they returned to the temple to find, to their surprise, that the light was still burning.

"This is a miracle indeed!" one villager shouted. "This must be God's work," another said. The Jewish people thanked God for the miracle of the oil lamp and for saving them from the wicked king.

Festival of Lights

To celebrate the miracle of the burning oil lamp, Jewish people light eight candles on a menorah. A new candle is lit on every day of the eight-day festival, until all of the candles are burning.

The light from the menorah is used to celebrate Jewish people's faith in God. It is used to show that God is always there to guide them in both good and bad times.

Jacob says:
MEN-OR-AH
(Menorah)

The ninth candle in the middle of a menorah is used to **light the other eight candles.**

Jacob says:
BIRR-CAT HAM-A-ZON
(Birkat Hamazon)

Prayer and Worship

During Hanukkah religious ceremonies are held by rabbis in the synagogue. Jewish people read out parts of the Torah and worship God through prayer.

Worship also takes place at home. Jewish people usually read aloud a prayer called Birkat Hamazon after every meal. The prayer thanks God for his goodness and the food the family has been blessed with.

Playing Games

One of the most popular games played during Hanukkah is the dreidel game. A dreidel is a spinning top with a letter painted on each of its sides.

Children play by spinning the dreidel and guessing which letter it will fall on. Whoever guesses the letter correctly wins a "pot of gelt." This is usually chocolate coins covered in silver and gold foil.

Jacob says:
DREY-DEL
(Dreidel)

Festive Food

Foods cooked in oil are eaten to remember the story of Hanukkah and the oil lamp. Flat, fried potato pancakes, called latkes, are traditionally eaten during Hanukkah.

Sweet foods, like sufganiyot, are also eaten during the festival. Sufganiyots are round jelly doughnuts, fried in oil and sprinkled with a sugary icing.

Jacob says:
SOOF-GAN-I-YOT (Sufganiyot)
LAT-KEYS (Latkes)

Gifts, Family and Friends

Jewish children are often given gifts for each of the eight days of Hanukkah. Sweet foods, such as chocolate coins and candy, are popular gifts at this time of year.

Although Jewish people celebrate their faith in God during the festival, Hanukkah is also about spending time with family, friends and loved ones.

Jacob Says . . .

Anthiochus
ANT-I-OKE-US
Anthiochus was a great Greek king.

Birkat Hamazon
BIRR-CAT HAM-A-ZON
Birkat Hamazon is a prayer read after every meal.

Dreidel
DREY-DEL
A spinning top with four sides marked with a different Hebrew letter, used to play a game on Hanukkah.

Hanukkah
HAN-U-KAH
Hanukkah is a Jewish festival.

Latkes
LAT-KEYS
Latkes are fried potato pancakes.

Maccabees
MAC-A-BEES
The Maccabees are a group of people who fought against King Anthiochus.

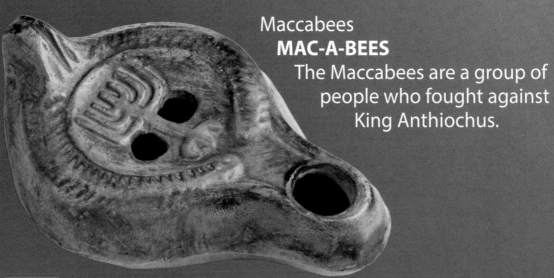

Menorah
MEN-OR-AH
A menorah has nine candles on it which are lit during Hanukkah.

Rabbi
RAB-EYE
A Jewish scholar, teacher, or religious leader.

Sufganiyot
SOOF-GAN-I-YOT
Sufganiyot are round jelly doughnuts, fried in oil and sprinkled with a sugary icing.

Synagogue
SIN-A-GOG
A synagogue is a Jewish place of worship.

23

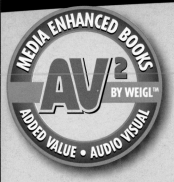

Log on to www.av2books.com

AV² by Weigl brings you media enhanced books that support active learning. Go to www.av2books.com, and enter the special code found on page 2 of this book. You will gain access to enriched and enhanced content that supplements and complements this book. Content includes video, audio, weblinks, quizzes, a slide show, and activities.

AV² Online Navigation

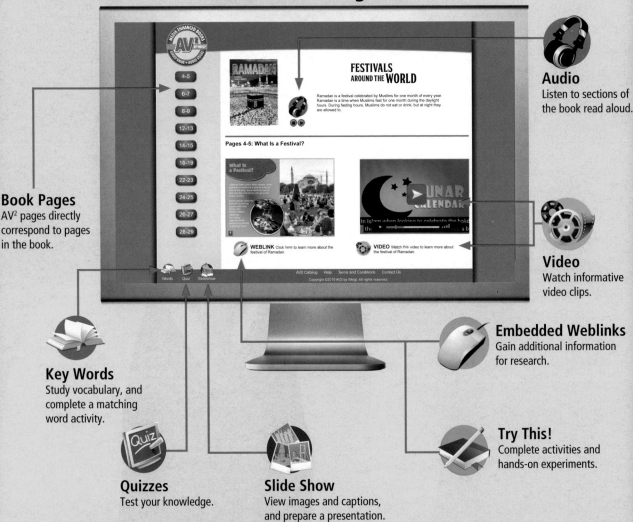

Audio
Listen to sections of the book read aloud.

Book Pages
AV² pages directly correspond to pages in the book.

Video
Watch informative video clips.

Key Words
Study vocabulary, and complete a matching word activity.

Embedded Weblinks
Gain additional information for research.

Quizzes
Test your knowledge.

Slide Show
View images and captions, and prepare a presentation.

Try This!
Complete activities and hands-on experiments.

AV² was built to bridge the gap between print and digital. We encourage you to tell us what you like and what you want to see in the future.

Sign up to be an AV² Ambassador at www.av2books.com/ambassador.